DECONSTRUCTING POWERFUL SPEECHES
ABRAHAM LINCOLN
THE GETTYSBURG ADDRESS

REBECCA SJONGER

CRABTREE
PUBLISHING COMPANY
WWW.CRABTREEBOOKS.COM

CRABTREE
PUBLISHING COMPANY
WWW.CRABTREEBOOKS.COM

Author:
Rebecca Sjonger
Series research and development:
Janine Deschenes and Ellen Rodger
Editorial director:
Kathy Middleton
Editor:
Ellen Rodger
Proofreader:
Wendy Scavuzzo
Graphic design:
Katherine Berti
Image research:
Rebecca Sjonger and Katherine Berti
Print and production coordinator:
Katherine Berti

Images:
Alamy: North Wind Picture Archives: p. 40
  Pictorial Press Ltd: p. 36–37
  White House Photo: p. 31
Granger, Sarim Images: front cover
Library of Congress: p. 6 (bottom), 8 (bottom right cover),
  9 (top right), 10, 15
  Painted by M. Wight; Engraved by H. Wright Smith: p. 5 (top right)
Shutterstock: Kristi Blokhin: p. 7 (center right)
  Paul Philippoteaux: p. 4–5
  Valerii Iavtushenko: p. 24
Wikimedia: p. 33 (top left)
  Adam Cuerden: p. 25
  arindambanerjee: p. 41 (top)
  Christies Lot Finder entry 5176324: p. 6 (top)
  Christophe Cagé: p. 32–33 (bottom)
  Engraving by W. Roberts: p. 21
  Heritage Auctions: p. 39 (top)
  John Gress Media Inc: p. 42
  Júlio Reis: p. 16
  Library of Congress Rare Book and Special
    Collections Division: p. 38
  Miscellaneous Items in High Demand, PPOC,
    Library of Congress: p. 34–35
  National Archives and Records Administration:
    p. 33 (top right)
  Smithsonian Exhibition: p. 11
  US Capitol, John Trumbull: p. 18–19
  US Senate, Art & History Home, First Reading of the
    Emancipation Proclamation by President Lincoln:
    p. 20–21
  White House, Pete Souza: p. 13
All other images by Shutterstock

Library and Archives Canada Cataloguing in Publication

Sjonger, Rebecca, author
        Abraham Lincoln : the Gettysburg Address /
Rebecca Sjonger.

(Deconstructing powerful speeches)
Includes bibliographical references and index.
Issued in print and electronic formats.
ISBN 978-0-7787-5238-7 (hardcover).--
ISBN 978-0-7787-5253-0 (softcover).--
ISBN 978-1-4271-2182-0 (HTML)

        1. Lincoln, Abraham, 1809-1865. Gettysburg address--Juvenile
literature. 2. Speeches, addresses, etc., American--Juvenile literature.
3. United States--History--Civil War, 1861-1865--Juvenile literature.
I. Title.

E475.55.S56 2019   j973.7'349   C2018-905557 X
                                          C2018-905558-8

Library of Congress Cataloging-in-Publication Data

Available at the Library of Congress

Crabtree Publishing Company
www.crabtreebooks.com   1-800-387-7650

Printed in the U.S.A./012019/CG20181123

**Published
in Canada
Crabtree Publishing**
616 Welland Ave.
St. Catharines, Ontario
L2M 5V6

**Published in the
United States
Crabtree Publishing**
PMB 59051
350 Fifth Avenue, 59th Floor
New York, New York 10118

**Published in the
United Kingdom
Crabtree Publishing**
Maritime House
Basin Road North, Hove
BN41 1WR

**Published
in Australia
Crabtree Publishing**
3 Charles Street
Coburg North
VIC 3058

CONTENTS

Address delivered at the cemetery at Gettysburg.

Four score and seven year[s]
brought forth on this conti[nent a new na]-
tion, conceived in Liberty, a[nd dedicated]
to the proposition that a[ll men are cre]-
ated equal.

Now we are engaged in a [great civil war,]
testing whether that nat[ion, or any nation]
so conceived and so ded[icated, can long]
endure. We are met on a g[reat battle-field]
of that war. We have come [to dedicate a]
portion of that field, as [a final resting]
place for those who here [gave their lives]
that that nation might [live. It is alto]-
gether fitting and proper [that we should]
do this.

But, in a larger sense, [we can not dedi]-
cate— we can not consecrat[e— we can not]
hallow— this ground. T[he brave, liv]-
ing and dead, who strug[gled here, have con]-
secrated it, far above ou[r]

INTRODUCTION

AMONG THE FALLEN

Gravediggers were still burying men in the cemetery on the day it opened in late fall, 1863. Just four months earlier, the site was a battlefield in the **American Civil War**. The bloody **Battle of Gettysburg** was fought from July 1 to 3. More than 10,000 soldiers were dead by the time it was over. Another 30,000 were injured.

In the weeks that followed, the small town of Gettysburg, Pennsylvania, was overwhelmed. Many of the dead had just been buried, some in shallow graves until other plans could be made. The sights and smells were awful.

About 3,500 fallen soldiers from the **Union army** were moved to the new cemetery. Of the **Confederates**, who lost the battle, 3,900 were left in their graves around the town for many years to come.

On November 19, a ceremony officially opened the Soldiers' National Cemetery. A parade of people walked from the town to the burial ground. Military bands marched along with them. Important public figures rode there on more than 100 horses. One of them was President Abraham Lincoln. Along with a new black suit and white gloves, he wore his usual stovepipe hat.

A scene from The Gettysburg Cyclorama of Pickett's Charge, a Confederate attack on July 3, 1863. French artist Paul Philippoteaux created this enormous panoramic painting to be displayed for crowds at the 1883 World's Fair.

More than 10,000 people were at the cemetery on that chilly morning. This included everyone from the families of the dead to state governors. Several people were invited to speak at the solemn event. When these men arrived, they sat on a platform so they could be seen. The audience crowded around them. Beyond them were the graves of the fallen soldiers.

In addition to the speakers, military bands played and prayers were said for the dead. The main part of the program was an **address**, or speech, given by Edward Everett. He was a well-known politician and **orator** from Massachusetts. Everett talked for two hours about the war and the Battle of Gettysburg. Long speeches like this were expected during that time period. Everett memorized every word of his address. When he was done, the audience gave Everett a long **ovation**.

Edward Everett was a politician, minister, and president of Harvard University in the 1800s.

TIMELINE

1860   November 6, Abraham Lincoln elected president of the United States

1860   December, South Carolina first of 11 southern states to withdraw from U.S.

1861   February, **Confederate States of America** forms and Jefferson Davis elected as its president

1861   March 4, President Lincoln takes office

1861   April, civil war between Confederate and Union armies breaks out

1863   July, Battle of Gettysburg

1863   November, Lincoln gives Gettysburg Addresss

1865   April, Lincoln killed

1865   May, civil war officially ends

A FEW MINUTES OF SPEECH

According to the program, the president was to make "dedicatory remarks" near the end of the ceremony. Since Everett was the main speaker, not much was expected from Lincoln. In fact, his speech was only a couple minutes long. This included pauses when the audience interrupted him with their clapping.

It was a totally different address from Everett's. Lincoln used the cemetery dedication to argue that the war was worth the huge loss of lives. Nothing less than the fate of the United States was at stake. In his Kentucky accent, Lincoln stated, "The world will little note, nor long remember what we say here." This did not turn out to be true. Lincoln's brief remarks became known as the Gettysburg Address.

Abraham Lincoln was the 16th president of the United States.

There are only two confirmed photographs of Lincoln at the site of the Gettysburg Address. Photography was new at the time, and images were sometimes blurry. Lincoln is visible in the top left of this photo.

Later, Everett wrote to Lincoln that he wished he "had come as near to the central idea of the occasion in two hours as you did in two minutes." Lincoln's speech was short, but he chose each word with great care. It is still quoted widely today. In fact, it is one of the most famous speeches in modern history. At the president's funeral, Senator Charles Sumner declared, "The world noted at once what he said, and will never cease to remember it. The battle itself was less important than the speech."

READ IT

To see the full text of Edward Everett's cemetery dedication speech, visit **https://bit.ly/2sIHtwD**

More than 6,000 soldiers are now buried at the cemetery in Gettysburg. The Gettysburg Address took place near the Soldiers' National Monument (shown here) that was completed in 1869.

Lincoln's Gettysburg Address Memorial

CHAPTER 1

PERSUASIVE PRIMARY SOURCES

The speech Abraham Lincoln made at Gettysburg is a primary source. These resources are original, firsthand accounts. The **U.S. Library of Congress** calls them "the raw materials of history." They include many kinds of images, video and audio files, and texts. Diaries, **oral histories**, and scrapbooks are just a few examples. Recorded facts such as the data from a birth certificate or in a government report are also primary sources. They bring us as close as we can get to being present at a certain time or event in history. The Gettysburg Address offers a view of the United States during the civil war in the 1860s.

A SECOND OPINION

Often, materials that focus on an event or time period are created many years later. These are secondary sources. They are a type of explanation called an **interpretation**. These sources may also state an opinion. Their purpose is to analyze, or study, one or more primary sources. They include journal articles, school textbooks, and entertainment reviews. Secondary sources can look at an event or issue in many ways. Some refer to other sources. This provides a broader view of what took place. They also offer context, which is helpful background information. This book is a secondary source that focuses on Lincoln's speech.

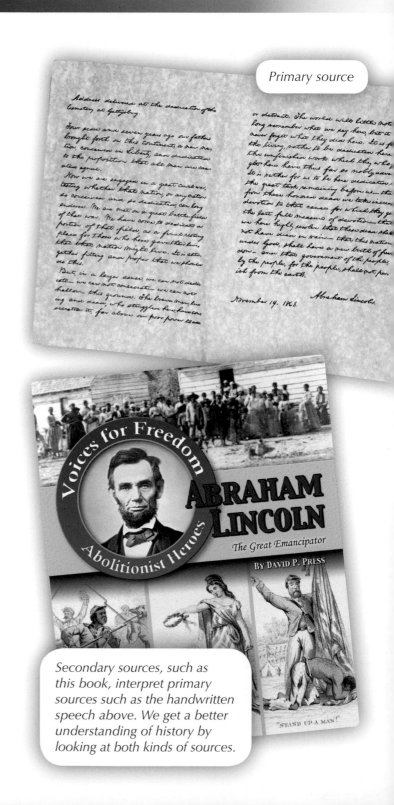

Primary source

Secondary sources, such as this book, interpret primary sources such as the handwritten speech above. We get a better understanding of history by looking at both kinds of sources.

SOURCE ANALYSIS 101

Checking the following facts will help determine if a primary source can be trusted. Gathering this information is the first step in analyzing a primary source.

Maker, such as a writer

Intended audience

Date it was created

NOVEMBER 19, 1863

Purpose

Place it was delivered

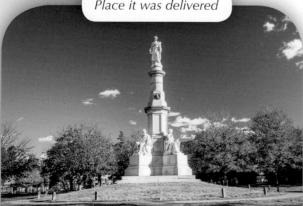

Maker's point of view

THE REAL DEAL

There are no video or audio recordings of speeches as old as the Gettysburg Address. Sometimes, a transcript, or handwritten log, of a speech is available to study. Luckily, President Lincoln wrote out his speech before delivering it. Lincoln gave what appears to be the first draft to his secretary, John G. Nicolay. It was started on paper from the White House and finished on different paper in Gettysburg. A revised draft was given to an assistant named John Hay. Both Nicolay and Hay were in the audience at the cemetery.

DIGGING DEEPER

The lack of recordings can make it difficult to prove what was really said in a historical speech. What potential problems could this pose?

The Library of Congress owns the two oldest copies of the Gettysburg Address.

Hay version

Nicolay version

ONE SPEECH, MANY COPIES

Abraham Lincoln also handwrote copies of his speech after the dedication. They were mainly used at events that raised funds for Union soldiers. Today, each version is named after the person who received the speech from Lincoln. For example, the Everett copy was given to Edward Everett. Five copies of the address still exist. This book uses the text Union Army Colonel Alexander Bliss received in 1864. It is the last known copy written by Lincoln himself.

Address delivered at the dedication of the Cemetery at Gettysburg.

Four score and seven years ago our fathers brought forth on this continent, a new nation, conceived in Liberty, and dedicated to the proposition that all men are created equal.

Now we are engaged in a great civil war, testing whether that nation, or any nation so conceived and so dedicated, can long endure. We are met on a great battle-field of that war. We have come to dedicate a portion of that field, as a final resting place for those who here gave their lives that that nation might live. It is altogether fitting and proper that we should do this.

But, in a larger sense, we can not dedicate— we can not consecrate— we can not hallow— this ground. The brave men, living and dead, who struggled here, have consecrated it, far above our poor power to add or detract. The world will little note, nor long remember what we say here, but it can never forget what they did here. It is for us the living, rather, to be dedicated here to the unfinished work which they who fought here have thus far so nobly advanced. It is rather for us to be here dedicated to the great task remaining before us— that from these honored dead we take increased devotion to that cause for which they gave the last full measure of devotion— that we here highly resolve that these dead shall not have died in vain— that this nation, under God, shall have a new birth of freedom— and that government of the people, by the people, for the people, shall not perish from the earth.

Abraham Lincoln.

November 19, 1863.

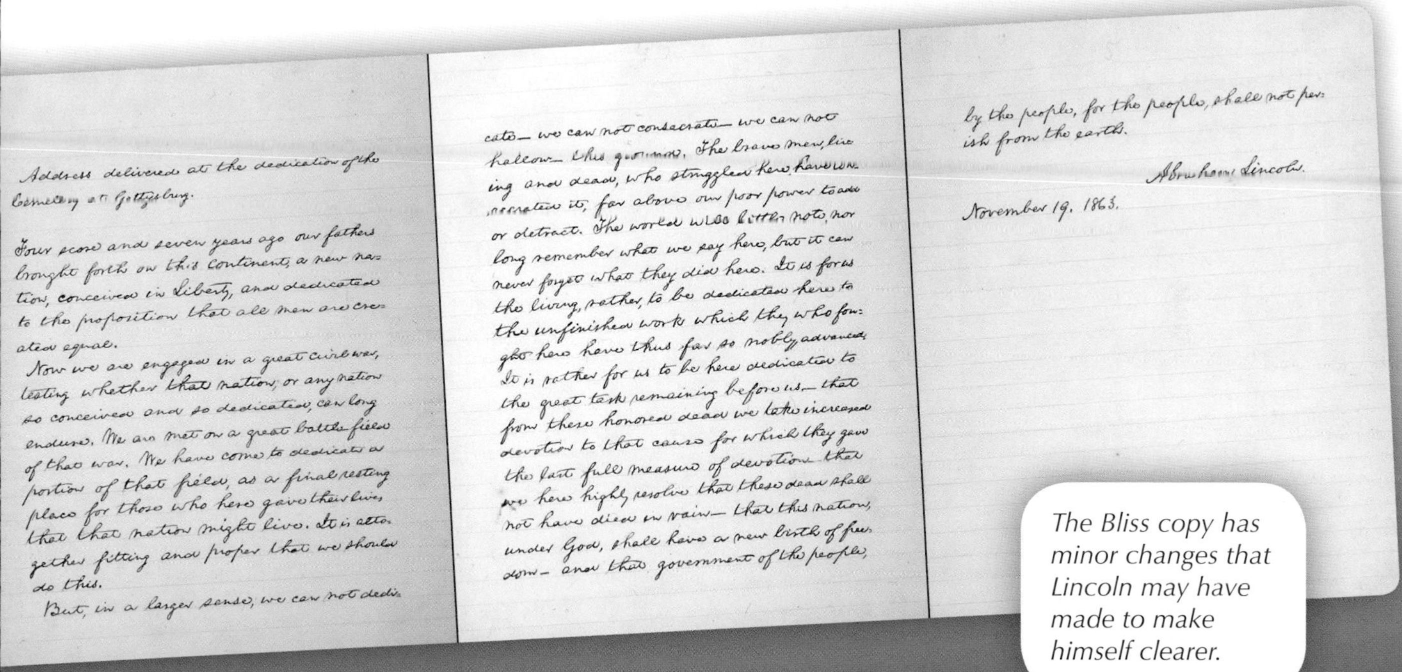

The Bliss copy has minor changes that Lincoln may have made to make himself clearer.

“*Abraham Lincoln*

November 19, 1863

Address delivered at the dedication of the cemetery at Gettysburg

***It is for us the living, rather, to be dedicated here to the unfinished work which they who fought here have thus far so nobly advanced.*”**

Maker

The Bliss copy of the speech is the only signed and dated version

Place of origin and intended audience

Lincoln's purpose is to encourage the *Union states* to continue fighting the Confederacy

FACTS FILES

As a former president of the United States, Abraham Lincoln is a major figure from history. Information about him and his speeches is widely available. This is not always the case with primary sources. The materials may not include the details needed to assess them. Museums and libraries gather as many details as they can. Whatever can be found is listed in catalogs, or **databases**. Checking them is often helpful when studying a speech.

A POWERFUL TOOL

The spoken word can be an effective way to push for change. Speeches such as President Lincoln's Gettysburg Address often present a specific point of view about one issue. They are crafted to sway an audience and encourage the audience to think a certain way. The goal is to gain the audience's support. A few common features are found in most **persuasive** speeches.

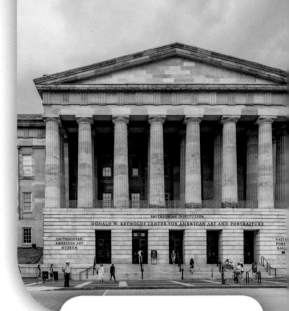

The Smithsonian Institution's collections include artifacts from Abraham Lincoln's life and his writings. The National Portrait Gallery has paintings, sketches, and photos of Lincoln. Other libraries and archives hold his speeches.

MAKING AN ARGUMENT

CLAIM

Speeches support their arguments with claims, which are statements or conclusions.

Everyone should brush their teeth.

WARRANT

Warrants connect claims and evidence to support a course of action.

Brushing teeth regularly helps people keep their teeth free of cavities.

EVIDENCE

Evidence is data or facts that prove the claims are true.

Not brushing teeth often leads to cavities.

APPEAL

Appeals in speeches urge the audience to act.

Brush your teeth after every meal!

Speechwriters take great care to choose just the right words to make an argument.

INFLUENCING THE AUDIENCE

Rhetoric is the art of persuasion used in speeches and many other texts. Rhetorical language convinces the audience using three main strategies.

LOGOS

Logos asks the audience to consider logic, or reason. In a speech, logos may begin with a general idea that is supported by facts. It could also use these facts as a starting point, then draw conclusions.

You should brush your teeth because it keeps your gums healthy, your breath fresh, and your teeth clean.

ETHOS

Ethos urges the audience to believe the speaker because of his or her good character. This may be done by sharing personal experiences, finding common ground, or showing respect.

As a dentist who fills cavities every day, I recommend brushing your teeth to stay out of my chair!

PATHOS

Pathos plays on the audience's emotions to win them over.

Do you want to wear false teeth someday because you didn't bother brushing your teeth?

WORDS THAT WORK

Speakers use rhetorical language in their own ways. It is backed by rhetorical devices, including:

- Using figurative language, such as **metaphors** and **similes**
- Comparing two different things in an **analogy**
- Repeating key words and phrases, such as "nation" in the Gettysburg Address
- Exaggerating in **hyperbole**
- Giving animals, objects, or ideas human qualities through **personification**
- Making some facts sound less important than they really are

HEARD NOT READ

Speechwriters expect their work to be heard. The experience is not the same when a speech is read silently. When read aloud, the language used and the speaker's voice and **inflections** work together to deliver the argument. The same words can be presented with very different effects, depending on how the speaker uses his or her voice.

THE POWER OF VOICE

The way someone pronounces and produces the sounds in words changes the ways audiences hear them. This is called diction. Diction also includes the words a speaker or writer chooses to use. Changing the tone in which words are said can transform the message. Imagine the phrase "Thanks a lot" said in a friendly way or with anger. The rising and falling rhythms of those tones are called cadence. Along with emphasis, all these things help speakers make their points.

Anyone can use rhetorical language to strengthen the claims, evidence, and warrants in their speeches.

NO RECORDINGS

Abraham Lincoln died shortly before the invention of the phonograph. It was one of the first recording devices. No one who is alive today has ever heard Lincoln's voice. Secondary sources note that people in the 1800s were surprised by how high-pitched it was. Some listeners found it took a while to get used to. Lincoln also had a strong Kentucky accent. No matter how his voice sounded, he was very thoughtful in how he presented his words.

Hearing Lincoln speak would have been a very different experience from reading his words.

DIGGING DEEPER

In Lincoln's speech, he says:

But, in a larger sense, we can not dedicate—we can not consecrate—we can not hallow—this ground.

How do you think he might have used rhythm, emphasis, and tone in this sentence?

CHAPTER 2

WORDS AND MEANING

Deconstructing a speech means analyzing it **critically** to determine its intended meaning. It also means examining other meanings imparted by language, the speechwriter's style and delivery (if known), and history. To analyze critically, begin by reviewing the whole source. Note how the information is presented. Then look for the parts of an argument and the rhetorical language described in the last chapter to understand how the speaker felt about the issue.

PRESENTING IDEAS

There are a few ways to present ideas in a speech. Placing them in order, especially with events, is called sequential listing. Lincoln does this when he starts with the past. He then refers to the ongoing civil war before looking to the future of the country. Placing them together for contrast in an argument is a type of comparative style.

The Gettysburg Address contrasts the living and the dead, for example. Speeches may also describe the reasons behind events, then the results. Using those facts is the cause-and-effect way of arranging information. Lincoln does this when he ties being "engaged in a great civil war" with "all men are created equal." He argues that the war cannot be avoided if the United States stands for equality.

PURPOSE

The purpose of a speech is the reason for making it. Lincoln had a goal at the Soldiers' National Cemetery dedication. He wanted to boost support for the Union army and its cause. Their victory at the Battle of Gettysburg had helped. However, the war was dragging on with no end in sight. The Confederate States of America had to be defeated so Lincoln could reunite the country.

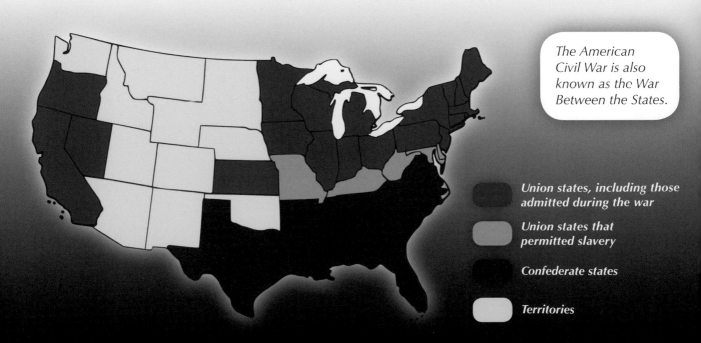

The American Civil War is also known as the War Between the States.

Union states, including those admitted during the war

Union states that permitted slavery

Confederate states

Territories

DECONSTRUCT IT

To determine the purpose of a speech, listen to it or read it and ask:
- What is the speaker's main argument?
- Who is the speaker trying to appeal to?

Speaker: President Abraham Lincoln
Audience: Soldiers, ordinary Americans, and dignitaries
Date: November 19, 1863

" *It is for **us** the living, rather, to **be dedicated** here to the **unfinished work** which they who fought **here** have thus far so **nobly advanced**.* "

The audience included government leaders, people who lived in the area, and families of soldiers who had died there
The event committed the land to its new use as a cemetery, but Lincoln urges Americans to dedicate themselves, too; forms of "dedicate" are repeated six times in this speech
Winning the war and reuniting the states
On the ground where everyone stood
Through the sacrifice of dying in battle; "advanced" suggests progress and victory

SPEAKER SPOTLIGHT

Five years earlier, Abraham Lincoln gave another famous address in Springfield, Illinois. It became known as the "House Divided" speech. More than 1,000 of his fellow Republicans were in the audience. Lincoln spoke to them about slavery and the future of the country. Most northern states did not allow slavery. The southern states relied on it. This disagreement was splitting up the United States. It led to the civil war and battles such as at Gettysburg.

Speaker: Abraham Lincoln (as Republican U.S. Senator nominee for Illinois)
Audience: Illinois Republican Party members at Springfield nomination
Date: June 16, 1858

" *A **house divided** against itself cannot stand. I believe this government cannot endure…**half slave** and half free.* "

Refers to the United States
State against state
Quotes a Bible passage used in a variety of ways over the centuries
Go on
The nation could not allow each state to have its own slavery laws

READ IT

See the full text of the "House Divided" speech at **www.abrahamlincoln online.org/lincoln/ speeches/house.htm**

CLAIMS AND EVIDENCE

The Gettysburg Address and other speeches back their arguments with claims. They show evidence that proves those claims are true. The kinds used depend on factors such as the audience, the time period, and the setting. The backdrop of the civil war-era cemetery helped form President Lincoln's claim and evidence. His solemn speech draws from the battle that took place there. He used his voice and pacing for emphasis.

DECONSTRUCT IT

To find claims and evidence in a speech, ask:
- What conclusions are being made?
- Which facts or data support these statements?
- Is the speaker using voice, such as emphasis or pacing, to reinforce any text?

Speaker: *President Abraham Lincoln*
Audience: *Soldiers, ordinary Americans, and dignitaries*
Date: *November 19, 1863*

The Declaration of Independence's emphasis on the equality of "all men" informed Lincoln's thoughts when he composed his Gettysburg speech. The declaration's drafting committee is shown here presenting their work to Congress.

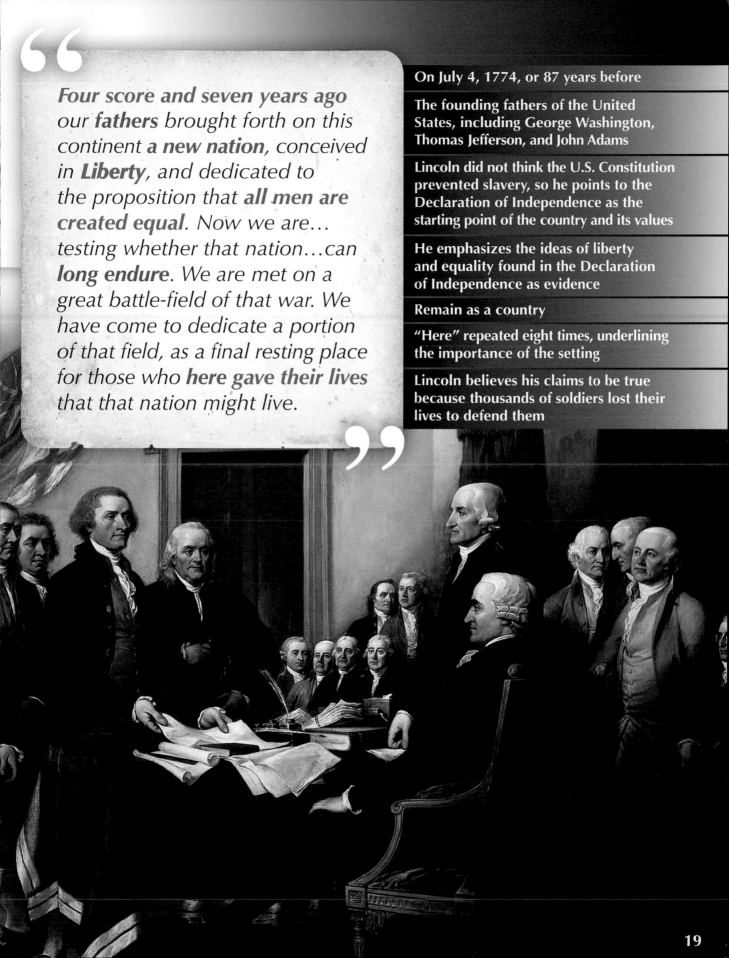

> *Four score and seven years ago* our **fathers** brought forth on this continent **a new nation**, conceived in **Liberty**, and dedicated to the proposition that **all men are created equal**. Now we are… testing whether that nation…can **long endure**. We are met on a great battle-field of that war. We have come to dedicate a portion of that field, as a final resting place for those who **here gave their lives** that that nation might live.

On July 4, 1774, or 87 years before
The founding fathers of the United States, including George Washington, Thomas Jefferson, and John Adams
Lincoln did not think the U.S. Constitution prevented slavery, so he points to the Declaration of Independence as the starting point of the country and its values
He emphasizes the ideas of liberty and equality found in the Declaration of Independence as evidence
Remain as a country
"Here" repeated eight times, underlining the importance of the setting
Lincoln believes his claims to be true because thousands of soldiers lost their lives to defend them

SPEAKER SPOTLIGHT

On January 1, 1863, President Lincoln took a step toward ending slavery in the United States. He made an order called the Emancipation Proclamation. It freed slaves who lived in the states that were at war with the Union. Lincoln's order gave evidence that claim of equality was true.

Source: *Emancipation Proclamation*
Audience: *Rebel states and entire nation*
Date: *January 1, 1863*

"

*...all persons held as slaves within any State... in rebellion against the **United States**, shall be... forever **free**...And I further declare and make known, that such persons of suitable condition, **will be received into the armed service of the United States**...*

"

Applies only to slaves in the Confederacy—not those in the Union

However, slaves living in these states would find it very difficult to receive this freedom

Lincoln wanted freed slaves to become soldiers in the Union forces

The Emancipation Proclamation was an executive order, which only a president can make.

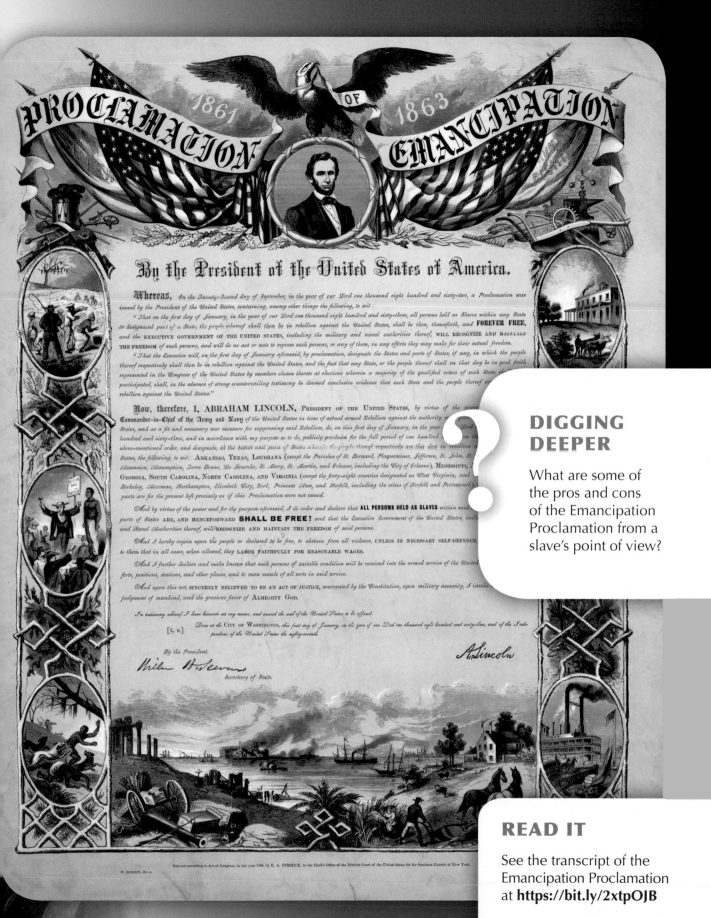

WARRANTS AND APPEALS

Appeals in speeches request action of some kind. Abraham Lincoln appeals to the audience at Gettysburg to dedicate themselves to reuniting the country. Warrants are statements that support this course of action. Lincoln connected his claims and evidence in warrants to justify the ongoing war.

DECONSTRUCT IT

Find warrants and appeals in a speech by asking:
- Is the speaker urging the audience to act or think a certain way?
- How are claims and evidence being connected to convince them?

> *It is rather for us to be here dedicated to the **great task** remaining before us…devotion to that **cause** for which they gave the **last full measure of devotion**—that we here highly resolve that these dead **shall not have died in vain**—that **this nation, under God**, shall have a **new birth** of freedom—and that government **of the people, by the people, for the people**, shall not **perish from the earth**.*

Winning the war
Reuniting all the states under the control of the federal government
Dying in battle
To give up fighting the war would mean their deaths were for nothing
Reflects the importance of the Christian belief system for people, despite the separation of church and state
Contrasts with the death of the soldiers
Lincoln may be quoting one of Theodore Parker's sermons from the late 1850s or the earliest known source, a 1384 Bible introduction written by John Wycliffe
Pass away
The people must take action to save the United States of America

EXPANDING THE MEANING

When Lincoln references "government of the people, by the people, for the people," historians note that he was borrowing a quote from a well-known Christian minister, Theodore Parker. Parker was an **abolitionist** whose sermons were very influential in the 1850s and supported building a fair and **just** society. His exact wording was "government of all the people, by all the people, for all the people," and he was speaking of democracy. To Parker, "all the people" referred to the fact that full democracy was not yet practiced in America.

Source: *Gettysburg Address*
Audience: *Soldiers, ordinary Americans, and dignitaries*
Date: *November 19, 1863*

SPEAKER SPOTLIGHT

President Lincoln made his second **inaugural** address as the war came to an end in 1865. He delivered it at the Capitol Building in Washington, D.C., on March 4. Lincoln believed this to be his greatest speech. In it, he appeals to the American people to come together and restore the country. Lincoln's speech concludes:

READ IT

To read Abraham Lincoln's second inaugural address, visit **www.bartleby.com/124/pres32.html**

Speaker: President Abraham Lincoln
Audience: Inaugural crowd
Date: March 4, 1865

> *With **malice toward none**; with **charity** for all; with **firmness in the right**…let us strive on to finish the **work we are in**; to **bind up the nation's wounds**; to care for him who shall have borne the battle, and for his widow, and his orphan—to do all which may achieve…a **lasting peace**…*

Example of Lincoln's repeated appeals for unity between the states and no thoughts of revenge
Providing help
The reunion of the states as one nation
Rebuilding the country after the war
The country is personified as one of the almost half a million wounded soldiers and the idea of healing wounds
Appeals for this never to happen again

Lincoln delivered the address just a month before he was assassinated. In it, he spoke of forgiveness and national **reconciliation**.

RHETORICAL LANGUAGE

Abraham Lincoln said a lot with just a few well-chosen words. His rhetoric included logos, ethos, and pathos, as well as devices that helped make his arguments. He used his authority as president and his well-known character. The emotional setting of the new cemetery also helped him.

DECONSTRUCT IT

To identify the rhetorical language in a speech, ask:
- How is the speaker using logic and reason to sway the audience?
- Does the speaker's character help support the central argument?
- How is the audience being swayed by emotion?

Lincoln predicted that slavery would be everywhere in the country or nowhere in the future.

Speaker: President Abraham Lincoln
Audience: Soldiers, ordinary Americans, and dignitaries
Date: November 19, 1863

*Four score and seven years ago our fathers brought forth…a new nation…dedicated to the proposition that **all men are created equal**. Now **we** are engaged in a great civil war…**We are met on a great battle-field of that war**. We have come to dedicate a portion of that field, as a final resting place for those who here gave their lives that that nation might live…*

Lincoln uses logos to point toward established facts

By using "we" throughout, Lincoln finds common ground in shared experience, which is ethos

Lincoln uses short, simple words to inspire the audience's trust in him

Pathos plays on the audience's emotions

SPEAKER SPOTLIGHT

Abraham Lincoln had great skill with rhetorical language. He used it when he delivered one of his earliest-known speeches, entitled "The Perpetuation of Our Political Institutions," at the Young Men's Lyceum in Springfield, Illinois, in winter 1838. This was 25 years before the Gettysburg Address. Lincoln was already a gifted speaker at the age of 28. He was also already concerned about the unity of the nation. In the months leading up to the speech, mobs had killed prominent abolitionists. Without mentioning the specific events (which his audience would have known) Lincoln addressed the idea of being wary of **mob rule** and the threat of America siding with an ambitious ruler who could **corrupt** the government.

A young Abe Lincoln, without his characteristic beard.

Speaker: *Abraham Lincoln*
Audience: *Mostly white men, and some women at a center for educational lectures*
Date: *January 27, 1838*

READ IT

To read Lincoln's "Perpetuation of Our Political Institutions" speech, visit: **https://bit.ly/2kxIki7**

> *...Shall **we** expect some transatlantic **military giant**, to step the Ocean, and crush us at a blow? Never! All the armies of Europe, Asia and Africa combined...with a **Buonaparte** for a commander, could not by force, take a drink from the **Ohio**, or make a track on the **Blue Ridge**, in a **trial** of a **thousand years**. At what point then is the approach of danger to be expected?...If it ever reach us, it must **spring up amongst us**...*

Ethos implies Lincoln and the audience are on the same side

Use of imagery

Refers to Napoleon, a famous European leader and *statesman*

River that flows through six states

Mountains in the Appalachians; imagery emphasizes American's natural resources

War

Uses pathos to whip up the crowd's emotions

Lincoln predicts that any risk to the United States will come from within

CHAPTER 3

ANALYZING PERSPECTIVES

Many of Abraham Lincoln's speeches promoted American unity. His arguments showed his own perspective, or point of view. Most speeches reveal how the writer feels about an issue. However, the writer of a speech and the speaker are not always the same person. Sometimes, a writer creates a speech on behalf of the person who gives it. The writer aims to present the speaker's perspective. Many politicians and statesmen today give hundreds of speeches and often have teams of speechwriters who help them. Abraham Lincoln wrote his own speeches, including the Gettysburg Address.

AMERICA IN THE 1800S

The time in history when a speech is made affects its perspective. Just as the arguments and language used reveal details about an era or event, the point of view shows what the world was like at the time. Both the speechmaker and the audience are products of their time. Looking back, it is easy to wonder why anyone had to argue against slavery. However, when Lincoln was alive, many Americans thought of slaves as their property. Even some of the founding fathers of the United States owned slaves. Over time, society's perspectives shifted slowly. Slavery was eventually abolished, or ended, but it took many years.

The labor of enslaved peoples helped enrich the nation.

DECONSTRUCT IT

To examine a speaker's perspective, ask:
- How does the language used show the speaker's feelings?
- How could the speaker's point of view be summed up in one sentence?

Source: *Gettysburg Address*
Audience: *Soldiers, ordinary Americans, and dignitaries*
Date: *November 19, 1863*

> *...a new nation... dedicated to the proposition that **all men are created equal**...The brave men, living and dead, who struggled here, have **consecrated it**...The world will little note, nor long remember what we say here, but **it can never forget what they did here**...this nation, under God shall have a new birth of freedom...*

Lincoln's perspective is that the country itself is committed to equality

Set it apart for a higher purpose, suggesting Union soldiers are fighting for a just cause

Underscores Lincoln's view that the actions of the men who died in battle should not be dismissed or forgotten

This highlights the Christian point of view at the time and shows the high value for liberty in the United States

DIGGING DEEPER

Do you think a speechwriter and a speaker need to share the same point of view? Why or why not?

LINCOLN'S OUTLOOK

As president of the United States, Abraham Lincoln believed it was his job to keep the new nation together. The Confederate states in the South believed in the necessity and right to form their own country. Lincoln's perspective was that they had no right to break away. It was his point of view that the **secession** of the southern states was a threat to liberty and democracy.

Lincoln became president of the United States less than six weeks before the civil war broke out. His inaugural address in Washington was on March 4, 1861.

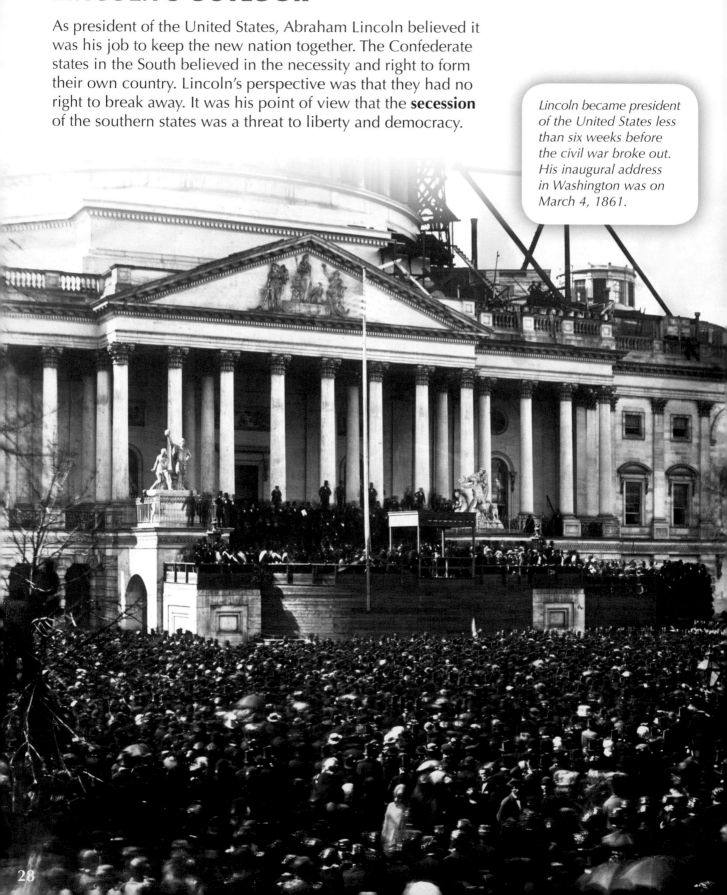

APPEAL TO THE SOUTH

Abraham Lincoln shared his perspective in his first inaugural address. He gave this speech when he became president in March 1861. Lincoln appealed to the South. He focused on those states that had recently seceded, or broken away, from the Union. They were not convinced. On April 12, Confederate soldiers attacked Fort Sumter. This act sparked the American Civil War.

DECONSTRUCT IT

To find the limitations of a speech, ask:
- How does the maker's perspective shape this primary source?
- Based on evidence from other sources, are there any points that should be explored further?

Speaker: *President Abraham Lincoln*
Audience: *Crowds gathered at his first inauguration*
Date: *March 1861*

READ IT

See copies of the Articles of Confederation and Perpetual Union Between the States at **https://bit.ly/2RV3ofY**

> *I hold that…**the Union of these States is perpetual**…it being impossible to destroy it except by some action not provided for in the **instrument** itself… no State upon it's own mere motion can lawfully get out of the Union; that **resolves and ordinances to that effect** are legally void, and that **acts of violence within any State or States against the authority of the United States** are **insurrectionary or revolutionary**…*

In the Articles of Confederation, which came into effect in 1781, the original 13 states agreed to a never-ending union

The U.S. Constitution

Laws and orders during the time that Alabama, Florida, Georgia, Louisiana, Mississippi, South Carolina, and Texas had seceded

Relates to rising up against the government

Relates to promoting a rebellion

SELECTIVE FACTS

Speeches and other primary sources often present only one perspective about an issue. This limits what can be learned from them. President Lincoln's goal was to restore the Union. To make his argument, Lincoln might have left certain facts out of the Gettysburg Address. He chose evidence that made his claims and warrants stronger. Some secondary sources argue that his emphasis on equality was self-serving. It appealed to freed slaves with the goal of building up the Union army. (Flip back to page 20 to read about the Emancipation Proclamation.) Lincoln was against slavery. However, in his point of view, the Constitution allowed it. This fact does not appear in the speech.

HONEST ABE?

In the Gettysburg Address, Abraham Lincoln argues for equality. However, in notes from speeches he made in Kansas and Ohio in September 1859, he wrote, "We must not disturb slavery in the states where it exists, because the Constitution, and the peace of the country both forbid us…" In his first inaugural address, he claimed, "I have no purpose, directly or indirectly, to interfere with the institution of slavery in the States where it exists. I believe I have no lawful right to do so, and I have no inclination to do so." More than a year into the civil war, Lincoln wrote *New-York Tribune* editor Horace Greeley. Lincoln stated (below):

(Flip back to page 20 to read about the Emancipation Proclamation.)

DIGGING DEEPER

President Lincoln did not mention the enormous number of deaths caused by the Battle of Gettysburg. What reasons might he have had not to refer to them?

DIGGING DEEPER

Do you think the Gettysburg Address contradicts any of Lincoln's other speeches? How might fighting the civil war have changed Lincoln's point of view?

> *If I could save the Union without freeing any slave, I would do it, and if I could save it by freeing all the slaves, I would do it, and if I could save it by freeing some and leaving others alone, I would also do that.*

Lincoln believed that keeping the United States together was the most important goal.

WORDPLAY STIRS EMOTIONS

Using certain words can help create a feeling that sways the audience. This is called nuanced language. These word choices also reveal the speechmaker's perspective. Thanks to the multiple copies of the Gettysburg Address, we can see slight changes that Lincoln thought were important to make. For example, the Bliss copy changed "carried on" to "advanced" at the end of this sentence: "…to the unfinished work which they who fought here have thus far so nobly advanced." The new word emphasizes making progress instead of continuing as things are.

OTHER PERSPECTIVES

Abraham Lincoln and other speechmakers are not the only ones with a point of view. The people who create secondary sources have their own biases and perspectives. This can lead to multiple analyses of the same speech. It is important to study other primary and secondary sources to better understand an issue. These materials could be from the same time period or in response to the speech. Studying them can show what is missing.

The Bliss copy of the Gettysburg Address is on display in the Lincoln Bedroom at the White House.

THE OTHER GOVERNMENT

The Confederate States of America did not consider Abraham Lincoln to be their president. Their new government had its own leaders. Their perspective was very different from Lincoln's. Vice President Alexander H. Stephens's "Cornerstone Speech" reveals the Confederate point of view. Stephens gave it a few weeks before the start of the war in Savannah, Georgia.

The Confederate states used several versions of this flag to represent their new nation.

Speaker: Confederate States of America Vice President Alexander H. Stephens
Audience: White voters at the Athenaeum in Savannah, Georgia
Date: March 21, 1861

READ IT

To see the full text of the "Cornerstone Speech," visit **https://bit.ly/2PDFZ10**

*...**This revolution** has been... accomplished without the loss of a single drop of blood...its **cornerstone** rests, upon the great truth that the **negro is not equal to the white man**...The **process of disintegration in the old Union may be expected to go on with almost absolute certainty** if we pursue the right course... Why cannot the **whole question** be settled, if the north desire peace, simply by the Congress, in both branches, with the concurrence of the President, **giving their consent to the separation**, and a recognition of our independence?*

Seven states leaving the union in the previous three months
The name of the speech and a Christian reference to the Bible passage "the stone that the builders reject will be the cornerstone" to build upon
Language of the time not used today
The Confederacy's perspective in 1861
The opposite of Lincoln's perspective
Of the right to leave the United States
They saw no need for war if the South would be allowed to form a new confederacy

Alexander Stephens stayed in politics after the civil war. He was the governor of Georgia when he died in 1883.

Jefferson Davis was president of the Confederate States of America from 1861 until 1865.

The first battle in the civil war took place at Fort Sumter. The fort stood in the harbor of Charleston, South Carolina.

33

AN ABOLITIONIST'S POINT OF VIEW

African American Frederick Douglass was an abolitionist, writer, and newspaper publisher who worked to end slavery. A formerly enslaved person, Douglass made many public speeches. On July 5, 1852, he spoke to more than 500 abolitionists in Rochester, N.Y. This famous speech offered a different take on the Declaration of Independence and slavery.

READ IT

View the transcript of the speech made by Frederick Douglass at **www.pbs.org/wgbh/aia/part4/ 4h2927t.html**

Speaker: *Frederick Douglass*
Audience: *The Rochester Ladies' Anti-Slavery Society, Rochester, N.Y.*
Date: *July 5, 1852*

> *What, to the American slave, is your **Fourth of July**? I answer; a day that reveals to him…the **gross injustice and cruelty to which he is the constant victim**. To him, your celebration is a sham… **your shouts of liberty and equality, hollow mockery**…mere bombast, fraud, deception, impiety and **hypocrisy**—a thin veil to cover up crimes which would disgrace a nation of **savages**. **There is not a nation on the earth guilty of practices more shocking and bloody than are the people of the United States, at this very hour**.*

The date of the signing of the Declaration of Independence, which Americans celebrate as Independence Day
Refers to the terrible treatment of enslaved persons and free blacks
Compare to how Lincoln refers to liberty and equality
When someone's words and actions do not match
Plays on slaveholders' use of the word "savages" to describe blacks
At the time, more than three million people worked long days without pay and were denied liberty and humane treatment as enslaved persons in America

Frederick Douglass was a featured speaker at an abolitionist meeting in Tremont Temple in Boston. Held shortly after Lincoln was elected in 1860, the meeting was shut down when anti-abolitionists disrupted it and called the police.

Frederick Douglass learned to read as a child by trading scraps of food for lessons. He later escaped slavery and became a leader in the abolitionist movement.

FIGHTING FOR EQUALITY

The states were reunited after the civil war ended. However, the statement that "all men are created equal" was continually challenged. Racial segregation separated people based on the color of their skin. In the 1950s and 1960s, the civil rights movement fought for equality. One of the era's greatest leaders was Martin Luther King, Jr. In late August 1963, he argued against racial inequality in front of 250,000 people in Washington. This famous speech is known as "I Have a Dream."

Speaker: *Martin Luther King, Jr.*
Audience: *Civil rights marchers (250,000) gathered at the Lincoln Memorial in Washington, D.C., during the March on Washington for Jobs and Freedom*
Date: *August 28, 1963*

*I have a dream that one day this nation will rise up and live out the true meaning of its creed: 'We **hold these truths to be self-evident, that all men are created equal.**' I have a dream that one day out on the red hills of **Georgia sons of former slaves and the sons of former slave-owners will be able to sit down together at the table** of brotherhood.*

Wording from the Declaration of Independence

A former Confederate state

The idea of sitting together in equality was still only a dream a century after the civil war

EXPANDING THE MEANING

King's speech was one of many delivered on that day. It began with a nod to the crowd and how the event would go down in the country's history as the greatest demonstration for freedom. King also chose to begin the speech with a reference to Lincoln's famous "Four score" introduction in the Gettysburg Address: "Five score years ago a great American in whose symbolic shadow we stand today signed the Emancipation Proclamation." Like Lincoln, King wrote his own speeches, and in "I Have a Dream" references the American ideals of justice and liberty and the freedoms **enshrined** in the Constitution and the Declaration of Independence.

READ IT

The Martin Luther King, Jr. Research and Education Institute at Stanford University has the full text and an audio file of the "I Have a Dream" speech at **https://stanford.io/1FqpWGi**

DIGGING DEEPER

Do you think everyone is treated as equals in your school or your community? Why or why not?

CHAPTER 4

INFLUENCES THEN AND NOW

Many newspapers ran President Lincoln's speech the day after the cemetery dedication. This widened its audience across the country. Most of his supporters thought it was a powerful speech. However, his enemies agreed with Lincoln himself that it would soon be forgotten.

LASTING IMPACT

Abraham Lincoln's supporters were proven correct. More than 150 years later, the Gettysburg Address is still well known. Back in 1863, it met its purpose of boosting wartime efforts. The Battle of Gettysburg victory and Lincoln's speech helped drive the Union cause forward. The American Civil War finally ended in spring 1865.

A SHOCKING DEATH

The war claimed more than 620,000 lives. One more life was lost on April 14, 1865. John Wilkes Booth shot President Lincoln at Ford's Theatre in Washington, D.C. Booth supported the Confederacy. A few days earlier, Booth heard Lincoln speak at the White House. The speech was about reuniting the states. Lincoln also talked about giving some African Americans the right to vote. Witnesses claimed that Booth said, "That is the last speech he will ever make." It turned out to be true. After killing Lincoln, Booth shouted, "The South is avenged!"

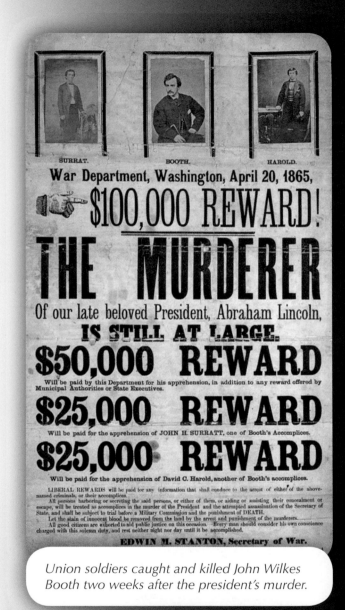

Union soldiers caught and killed John Wilkes Booth two weeks after the president's murder.

READ IT

To read the text of President Lincoln's final speech, visit **https://bit.ly/2FZOgqu**

Lincoln was shot at Ford's Theatre while watching a play, and slumped over in his chair. The assassin escaped by jumping off the balcony.

Lincoln's funeral train brought his body from Washington D.C., to Springfield, IL, with stops for public viewings, including here in Chicago.

CARRYING ON A LEGACY

Abraham Lincoln is remembered as one of the nation's greatest presidents. The Gettysburg Address is thought to be one of his best speeches. The five known copies handwritten by Lincoln himself are saved as national treasures. The U.S. Library of Congress owns the Nicolay and Hay copies. The Everett copy is at the Abraham Lincoln Presidential Library and Museum. Cornell University owns the Bancroft copy. The Bliss copy is displayed in the Lincoln Bedroom at the White House.

A CHANGING COUNTRY

The 13th Amendment to the Constitution ended slavery in the United States. It came into effect on December 6, 1865. Five years later, the 15th Amendment gave every male citizen the right to vote, no matter their race. However, many states resisted it with roadblocks such as **poll taxes**. It was not until the Voting Rights Act of 1965 that all African Americans were able to vote. They were not the only American citizens who fought for equality. People from Indigenous and Asian backgrounds faced similar racism at the time.

DIGGING DEEPER

If you knew about the Gettysburg Address before reading this book, has analyzing it changed how you think about it?

CHECK IT OUT

Visit **www.learntheaddress. org/#LO-jRBSj6vI** to see Americans from many backgrounds reciting the Gettysburg Address.

The House of Representatives was said to have erupted in relief when the 13th Amendment was passed.

IN THIS TEMPLE
AS IN THE HEARTS OF THE PEOPLE
FOR WHOM HE SAVED THE UNION
THE MEMORY OF ABRAHAM LINCOLN
IS ENSHRINED FOREVER

The text of the Gettysburg Address and President Lincoln's second inaugural speech are on the walls of the Lincoln Memorial.

A MODERN PRESIDENT'S PERSPECTIVE

The first African American president, Barack Obama, took office in 2009. Four years later, the United States marked the 150th anniversary of the Gettysburg Address. President Obama wrote a tribute in honor of it. This handwritten essay touched on the trials the nation had faced since the civil war. It was carefully crafted to be brief and handwritten like Lincoln's speech.

Speaker: *President Barack Obama*
Audience: *American public*
Date: *November 19, 2013*

DIGGING DEEPER

President Obama's tribute brings up the fight for rights by several groups. How does this reveal the ways perspectives in American society have changed since 1863?

Barack Obama drew inspiration from Abraham Lincoln for several of his important speeches.

READ IT

President Obama's reflection on the Gettysburg Address is available at **https://bit.ly/2sjbX98**

*…I linger on **these few words** that have helped define our American experiment: 'a new nation, conceived in liberty, and dedicated to the proposition that all men are created equal'…even a **self-evident truth was not self-executing**; that **blood drawn by the lash** was an **affront** to our **idealism**; that **blood drawn by the sword** was in painful service to those same ideals. **He** understood…it is through the accumulated toil and sacrifice of ordinary men and women—those like the **soldiers who consecrated that battlefield**—that this country is built, and freedom preserved…it falls to each generation, collectively, to share in that toil and sacrifice. Through **cold war** and **world war**, through **industrial revolutions** and **technological transformations**, through **movements for civil rights** and **women's rights** and **workers rights** and **gay rights**, we have. At times, social and economic changes have strained our union. But Lincoln's words give us confidence that whatever trials await us, this nation and the **freedom we cherish can, and shall, prevail**.*

Found in the Bliss copy of the Gettysburg Address on display at the White House	
Something that is clear to today's society	
It took a war to accomplish it	
Whipping was a common way of punishing slaves	
Insult	
Equality of men	
During battle in the American Civil War	
Lincoln	
Uses Lincoln's language for soldiers who died in the Battle of Gettysburg	
Refers to conflict between the United States and U.S.S.R. that lasted from 1945 to 1991	
America fought in the First and Second World Wars	
The worldwide shift to the use of machinery	
Impact of modern devices such as computers	
The fight for true equality for African Americans	
American women did not get the right to vote until 1920	
Protecting the labor force	
Fighting to be able to marry and get the same benefits as every other citizen	
Like Lincoln in the Gettysburg Address, Obama ends with a note of hope for the future	

BIBLIOGRAPHY

INTRODUCTION

"10 Facts: Abraham Lincoln and the Gettysburg Address." Legacy. https://bit.ly/2yHj5P2

"Abraham Lincoln." HistoryNet. www.historynet.com/abraham-lincoln

"Abraham Lincoln Takes a National Role." United States Library of Congress. https://bit.ly/2ykY0Ky

Bell, Clyde. "What Happened to Gettysburg's Confederate Dead?" The Blog of Gettysburg National Military Park. July 26, 2012. https://bit.ly/2P1ulud

Carter, Stephen L. "Abraham Lincoln's Top Hat: The Inside Story." *Smithsonian Magazine*, November 2013.

"Civil War Timeline." National Park Service, U.S. Department of the Interior. March 25, 2015. https://bit.ly/1IhoBar

"Gettysburg National Cemetery." National Park Service, U.S. Department of the Interior. https://bit.ly/2pV30kD

Leith, Sam. *Words Like Loaded Pistols: Rhetoric from Aristotle to Obama*. New York: Basic Books, 2012.

"Abraham Lincoln: Rise to National Prominence." United States Library of Congress. https://bit.ly/2AdEKAh.

"Looking for Lincoln." PBS. January 12, 2009. www.pbs.org/wnet/lookingforlincoln

McNamara, Robert. "Abraham Lincoln and the Gettysburg Address." ThoughtCo. August 31, 2018. https://bit.ly/2RUq8N0

Thompson, Paul. "The Gettysburg Address." *This Is America*. June 30, 2003. https://bit.ly/2J6p8Bz

Trueman, C.N. "Causes of the American Civil War." The History Learning Site. November 11, 2018. https://bit.ly/2CL67Ep

Wills, Garry. "The Words That Remade America." *The Atlantic: The Civil War Issue*. https://bit.ly/2PxiOoJ

CHAPTER 1

Fahnestock, Jeanne. *Rhetorical Style: The Uses of Language in Persuasion*. New York: Oxford University Press, 2011.

Gambino, Megan. "Ask an Expert: What Did Abraham Lincoln's Voice Sound Like?" ASK Smithsonian. June 6, 2011. https://bit.ly/2pWSlWP

"Gettysburg Address." *Encyclopaedia Britannica*. November 12. www.britannica.com/event/Gettysburg-Address

"Primary Sources." University of California Irvine Libraries. https://bit.ly/2QWoaug

"Primary Sources: What Are They?" Teaching History. https://bit.ly/2coOGwF

"The Gettysburg Address." Abraham Lincoln Online. https://bit.ly/1bFJewr

"The Gettysburg Address." Smithsonian National Museum of American History. https://s.si.edu/1KtKlmF

Thomas, Susan. "Primary vs. Secondary Sources." BMCC Library. https://bit.ly/2OvE9CE

"Using Primary Sources." United States Library of Congress. www.loc.gov/teachers/usingprimarysources

Weida, Stacy, and Karl Stolley. "Using Rhetorical Strategies for Persuasion." Purdue Online Writing Lab. https://bit.ly/2OqM0Nj

CHAPTER 2

"Emancipation Proclamation." History. September 3, 2018. https://bit.ly/1UIoJn4

"House Divided Speech." Abraham Lincoln Online. https://bit.ly/1FBivyS

Kelley, Sara. "The Rhetoric of Lincoln's 'Gettysburg Address'" *University of Massachusetts Dartmouth English Department E-Journal*, December 2008. www1.umassd.edu/corridors/thirdessay257.html

Langley, James A. "Who coined 'government of the people, by the people, for the people'?" *The Washington Post*. March 31, 2017.

"The Emancipation Proclamation." The U.S. National Archives and Records Administration. https://bit.ly/2P4q1jl

"The Inaugural address of President Abraham Lincoln, delivered at the National Capitol, March 4th, 1865." The Gilder Lehrman Collection. https://bit.ly/2QSEtZ6

Weber, Jennifer L., and Warren W. Hassler. "American Civil War." *Encyclopaedia Britannica*. 25 July 2018. https://bit.ly/2AeA6SJ

White, Ronald C. "The Gettysburg Address: Much noted and long remembered." *Los Angeles Times*. November 17, 2013.

CHAPTER 3

Ambrose, Stephen E. "Founding Fathers and Slaveholders." *Smithsonian Magazine*, November 2002.

Censky, Abigail. "'What To The Slave Is The Fourth of July?' Frederick Douglass, Revisited." NPR. July 5, 2017. https://n.pr/2uqz4hb

"'Corner Stone' Speech." Teaching American History. https://bit.ly/1deFCoK

"Fort Sumter." History. September 11, 2018. https://bit.ly/1HJQKUi

"'I Have a Dream' Speech." History. August 21, 2018. www.history.com/topics/i-have-a-dream-speech

Lincoln, Abraham. "A Letter from President Lincoln: Reply to Horace Greely." *The New York Times*. August 24, 1862: 1.

"Martin Luther King's Most Famous Speech." Social Studies for Kids. https://bit.ly/2rwtcnS

Pruitt, Sarah. "5 Things You May Not Know About Lincoln, Slavery and Emancipation." History. September 21, 2012. https://bit.ly/191io1j

The Tavis Smiley Show. "Frederick Douglass: 'The Meaning of July Fourth for the Negro.'" National Public Radio, July 4, 2003.

CHAPTER 4

"15th Amendment to the U.S. Constitution." United States Library of Congress. https://bit.ly/1n74TQA

"Booth's Reason for Assassination." Teaching History. https://bit.ly/2hAeIwh

"Gettysburg Address." United States Library of Congress. https://bit.ly/1OhCcjH

"Ideas are always more than battles." Cornell University. https://bit.ly/2IZ2Kd3

"Lincoln's Assassination." Ford's Theatre. www.fords.org/lincolns-assassination

"Remembering Lincoln at Gettysburg." Cornell University. https://bit.ly/2OrI8QT

Schulman, Kori. "President Obama's Handwritten Essay Marking the 150th Anniversary of the Gettysburg Address." The White House: President Barack Obama Archives. November 19, 2013.https://bit.ly/2pY6VNG

"The Cold War Timeline." History on the Net. https://bit.ly/2QUObKf

LEARNING MORE

BOOKS

Armstrong, Jennifer. *The True Story Behind Lincoln's Gettysburg Address*. New York: Aladdin, 2013.

Butzer, C. M. *Gettysburg: The Graphic Novel*. New York: HarperCollins, 2008.

Olson, Kay Melchisedech. *The Gettysburg Address in Translation: What It Really Means*. North Mankato: Capstone, 2016.

WEBSITES

Primary and secondary sources combine in a presentation about the Gettysburg Address:
https://artsandculture.google.com/exhibit/wReow-98

Get information about the Gettysburg Address and Abraham Lincoln:
http://gettyready.org

Watch videos, a documentary, and learn more about the Gettysburg Address:
www.learntheaddress.org

Find out more about primary and secondary sources:
www.lib.uci.edu/introduction-primary-sources

GLOSSARY

abolitionist A person who supported and worked for the abolition, or legal ending, of slavery

address A speech written or directed to a specific group of people

American Civil War A war between the North, or northern states, and the South, or southern states from 1861–1865

analogy A similarity between two things from which a comparison is made

Battle of Gettysburg A civil war battle fought around the town of Gettysburg, Pennsylvania, on July 1–3, 1863. With an estimated 23,000–28,000 dead and wounded, it is often described as the war's turning point.

Confederate States of America A group of (originally 7, later 11) southern states that declared their secession, or withdrawal, from the United States of America in 1861, leading to civil war

Confederates Supporters of the Confederate States of America

corrupt Dishonest, crooked, or lacking integrity

critically Using skillful judgment of truth and merit

databases Collections of facts, information, and statistics

enshrined Cherished or held sacred

hyperbole Obvious and intentional exaggeration

inaugural Marking the beginning of something, such as a new government

inflections Modulations of voice or changes in its pitch or tone

interpretation An explanation or meaning provided for something

just Rightful, based on fairness, and guided by truth or justice

liberty Freedom from arbitrary or unlimited control or rule

metaphors Figures of speech in which a term or phrase is used to represent something else

mob rule The rule of a group of people that often involves playing on emotions and inspiring anger and rage instead of reasoned thoughts and actions

oral histories Historical information gathered using sound recordings of interviews with people who have firsthand knowledge of an event or time period

orator Someone who delivers a formal public speech

ovation A long and enthusiastic show of appreciation, often by applause

personification Giving human qualities to an animal, object, or idea

persuasive Convincing through appeal or reason

poll taxes Fixed sum or flat-rate taxes that everyone has to pay regardless of their ability or level of wealth

reconciliation To settle a quarrel or dispute and become friendly again

secession The action of formally withdrawing from membership in a federation, especially a political union

similes Figures of speech in which two things that are not alike are compared

statesman A person who shows great wisdom and skill in government or public affairs

Union army The army of the United States of America during the civil war

Union states The North, or northern states, which were also called the United States of America

U.S. Library of Congress The research library that serves the United States Congress. It is also the national library of the United States and has the largest library collection in the world

INDEX

ABOUT THE AUTHOR

Rebecca Sjonger is the author of more than 50 nonfiction books for young people. American history is one of her favorite subjects to write about. She loves the challenge of separating facts from fiction while researching.